hope
in the
morning

COURTNEY PEPPERNELL

Dream for the things you wish to see. Speak for the things you wish to change.

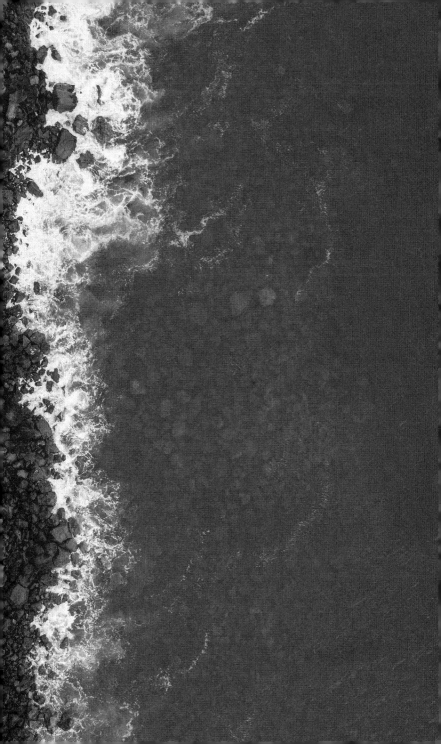

Listen Within

The seasons keep changing and the tides keep

washing the shore away. At the break of a new

day I am looking to my heart and listening to all

the things it has to say.

Courtney Peppernell

The earth is speaking

and we need to listen.

Courtney Peppernell

When I look at you, I am wondering about all

the things you are afraid to say. What moments

you keep hidden in between the folds and gentle

breaths of your heart. If by opening your heart

to my heart, perhaps you and I will share all

these lonely moments together.

Courtney Peppernell

We were under blankets, sleeping with the stars

above, whispering about all the things we should

have done. And you looked at me, with your

eyes dipped in moonlight and you promised we

would live our lives making memories out of

empty highways, and sunsets over mountains

and drifting in between oceans. My heart has

never been as full, as it was in that moment.

Courtney Peppernell

Let your heart
guide the way.
Listen within to
all the things it
has to say.

Courtney Peppernell

These memories all pull together like magnets

and hands finding eachother in the middle of

the night. I wish you knew how much I am

listening, to all your hopes and dreams and

insecurities. I wish you knew I'd stay awake all

night, just to watch to you sleep. How beautiful

you are to me, how you make me feel found,

even without uttering a sound.

Courtney Peppernell

Sometimes it is difficult when you believe so

deeply that you don't belong. When you feel like

the world is against you, and no one cares to

listen. You are awake in the middle of the night,

feeling alone, like a solitary planet, only ever

orbiting darkness. All you want is to leave, find

a safe space, where no one knows your name;

where you are free to start all over again. But

like the sun rising over hills in the morning light,

you too, will find your place. You too, will find

the strength in your heart and your safe space.

Courtney Peppernell

Your heart deserves to be cared for, to be

happy, to be nurtured and wanted and free.

Asking to be loved in the way that you love, is

never asking for too much. Sometimes you just

have to remind yourself, to ask the right people.

Courtney Peppernell

The walking away was never the hardest part. It

was the listening. Because for so long I had

refused to listen; to the people who cared about

me, to my head and to my heart. I had walked

blindly through the dark, ignored all the reasons

we were so bad for eachother. And the

listening took so much strength, so much

courage. To ask myself, where had I gone, when

had I become someone I had never wanted to

be. When had I stopped listening to my heart?

Courtney Peppernell

Create boundaries to protect your energy. Listen

to this energy. Surround yourself with the

people who match your inner intentions.

I hope one day you will sit down with your

sadness and listen to what it has to say.

Listening to your body, mind and soul is the

greatest act of courage that you will ever know.

Courtney Peppernell

You don't have to always know where life is

taking you. The current changes direction, the

clouds move and disappear, the stars shine a

little differently every night. But you should

listen to yourself, the direction you seek, where

you want to move and how you want to shine.

Courtney Peppernell

Acknowledge when your heart is hurting.

Breathe through the pain, know that it hurts,

but it will not break you.

The morning will cover you in light and from the darkness you will see the silver lining.

Come home to your heart.

Courtney Peppernell

You will learn to be bolder and braver. You will

learn that you are worth more than what people

may or may not say. You will learn that magic

runs in your very veins, and everything will be

okay no matter if the sky shines or it rains.

Courtney Peppernell

My heart turned to me and said, it is time to

listen. It is time to forgive the mistakes you have

made and the people who have let you down. It

is time to honor your strength and be at peace

with the times you have felt vulnerable. It is time

to say no to the things you don't want and to say

yes to the dreams you have. It is time to believe

in all the good you have done and will do. It is

time to realize that you deserve someone to love

you, and you deserve to love yourself.

Courtney Peppernell

you are emough

You are more than chasing someone who

doesn't see your light or worth. You are more

than settling for someone who doesn't realize

your wonder or acknowledge your truth. Chase

your dreams instead, run towards your goals, be

the best version of yourself you'll ever know.

Courtney Peppernell

They were not able to see your worth, and by

leaving, it does not mean you should question

whether you were enough but instead realize

that they weren't enough for you.

They did not deserve all you had to give.

Courtney Peppernell

You reached for me, landed between my sheets

and now the way your heart feels beating

against my chest, is the only thing in my head.

For as long as I live, I will love you with every

breath.

Courtney Peppernell

Every moment I am with you, barely feels like

enough. I want more and more moments with

you, because I think I'm falling in love.

Courtney Peppernell

All the things you feel, take time. They take

empathy and compassion and understanding.

This year, try to give yourself a little more of

each, even on the days you are falling apart.

Courtney Peppernell

Be with someone who inspires you to be more.

Who motivates you to achieve the things you

wish to achieve. Who wants the best for your

heart. Who reminds you that no matter where

you are or the road you are on, you'll always

and forever be enough.

Courtney Peppernell

Some of the most beautiful things in the world are here and have been accomplished because someone, somewhere, has never lost hope.

All the things I knew disapeared in those
moments when it felt like she had broken my
heart in two, when really she had shattered my
heart into a million tiny fragments. Memories
broken up and scattered all across my floor,
not really knowing what to do anymore. What
would happen, where would I go, when all that I
was had left, and all that I wanted to be, I didn't
know. I wondered why I wasn't good enough, or
smart enough or pretty enough. Why would she
want someone else instead of me. And in those
moments and the moments that came after, I
questioned my very soul. How one person could
do that, I still don't even know. But I did come
home and I did survive. And when the healing
was done, I understood why the pain had lived
on. To teach me that while it's okay to come
undone, the universe had always known best.
All along it was trying to tell me, that she had

never been the one.

Courtney Peppernell

You need to choose yourself sometimes. To step

away and open your arms to your own heart.

Courtney Peppernell

No one should ever make you question if you

are important enough to exist. No one should

ever make you question your worth, or if you

deserve love, compassion and kindness on this

earth. You deserve to be held and words

whispered in your ear, that you are loved and

you most certainly belong here.

Courtney Peppernell

You will come to know what drives you, what

inpires you and what you value most. And when

you do, don't compromise this for anyone or

anything.

Courtney Peppernell

I am hoping my love is
just enough, that you don't
ever think I'm too much.

Courtney Peppernell

There are so many people I pass every day, and

I don't speak to them and they don't speak to

me. I wonder if they are happy or sad, if they

have won everything or lost it all. So many

people and so much wonder.

I watched from the outside, the pretty stained

glass windows. How in the sunlight they would

glisten and glow, and when the sun set, the

darkness would creep in. But always could I

see a flicker of a flame inside. Always burning,

always lighting the window and the patterns

swirling across the glass. It was as though the

light inside still shone, despite the darkness.

This is how I feel about you; the way you glow

from within.

Courtney Peppernell

The universe knew you would find your way

back eventually. It knew not to give you more

than your heart could handle. It knew that you

would survive no matter the hurdles.

Courtney Peppernell

Maybe the kindest thing you'll say to yourself,

all day, all month and all year is -

I am enough and I am worthy to be here.

Courtney Peppernell

There is fear in the unknown and heartache when you feel alone. So put your best foot forward, and believe in the universe. Use your voice, surround yourself with people who have your best interests at heart, laugh often, do something new, don't worry about pleasing everyone, fall in love with the colors in the sky, whether they are pink or yellow or blue. Acknowlege life is always changing, like a rollercoaster, always up and down, sometimes simple, sometimes rough. Live every moment and love yourself, because you are truly and completely enough.

Courtney Peppernell

It won't matter if you are sixteen, thirty or

eighty-three, you will still have days that feel like

everything you've done and everything you've

hoped to be, doesn't matter. You will still feel as

though the world has no more purpose for you.

But whether you are sixteen or thirty or

eighty-three, know that you matter, that you are

beautiful, more than you believe and more than

you see.

Courtney Peppernell

run wild earth child

From time to time, one must leave their comfort

zone, to reach out into the unknown. To go

beyond what they thought they were capable of.

Courtney Peppernell

At the end of the day, an adventure is still an

adventure, even if it's sitting on your bedroom

floor, with a glass of wine, making lists of all the

goals you want to achieve.

I saw the galaxy
in her eyes,
the universe in
the curve of her
smile and I knew
more than anyone
she would
drive me wild.

You need to do what is best for you on any given

day. Stop worrying about unread texts or missed

phone calls. Stop inviting the people that never

show up. Stop keeping yourself from your own

heart.

There are moments I am homesick for the

places I have been. Not always for the people

there or the things that remain, but for the

person I was while there, and the person I will

now, never be again.

Courtney Peppernell

The world spins on an axis, always a little off

balance, always a little weirder than the day

before. Life is meant to keep moving. So keep

moving with it, and stay a little weird.

Courtney Peppernell

All she really wants is honesty and loyalty and a

little adventure.

It was never about the

destination or where we

would end up, as long as it

was your hand I was

holding and your face I could

see smiling.

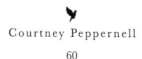

Courtney Peppernell

One day I hope you understand you were always

my favorite adventure.

Courtney Peppernell

All wonderful things come with struggle and

baggage. Life was never meant to be perfect.

The journey was never meant to be easy. But

every time it is difficult, remind yourself to

breathe, in the same way you breathed through

the struggle before. You survived then, and you

can certainly survive some more.

Courtney Peppernell

I don't want to arrive at the end of time

without ever really seeing someone. I don't want

to count how many times I didn't stop to truly

see someone's soul.

Courtney Peppernell

The person who turns up in an unexpected

moment, who cares for you deeply, who

cherishes your time together, who supports you

and doesn't try to change anything about you -

that is your most beautiful adventure.

Courtney Peppernell

Remember the journey you are taking and the

progress you have made. For every ounce of

doubt, remind yourself you have persisted. You

have climbed, you have ran, you have strived to

rebuild. From year to year, you can do anything

you set your mind to.

Courtney Peppernell

The journey continues when you decide to carry

on. When you decide to do the groceries, or

offer comfort to someone who needs it more

than you, or when you let the grief pass and the

sun shine. When you allow your heart from time

to time to still feel the rage and the despair but

it doesn't define you. When you let the love and

light back in. That is when your new journey

will begin.

Courtney Peppernell

Not every year or season will be monumental.

Some will be sadder or more difficult than

others. Some you will want to replay over and

over. But you must remember every season will

always belong to you, the good and the bad,

there is an entire universe inside of you.

Courtney Peppernell

There are many things that will return; flowers

in the spring, the sea to the shore, the birds to

the trees, the dust to the floor. But time never

returns. Once it passes, it is gone. Every second,

every minute, every hour and day. So use it with

intention and good will. Use it in the way you

won't regret. Use it, so that your time is fulfilled.

Courtney Peppernell

Be Kind

There are people who you can simply look at,

and see all the wonder, beauty and kindness in

the world.

Courtney Peppernell

The kindness and empathy you show to others,

not just in times of struggle, but times of joy as

well, will be your legacy.

Courtney Peppernell

Sometimes all we can do and all we can hope for is to hold onto each other as tightly as we can.

I know you feel like you do so much, that the

weight of the world is always on your

shoulders. I know you put others first and

sometimes other people's selfishness just doesn't

seem fair. I know that it is tiring to always want

the best for someone else and that you forget

about yourself. But you are seen and you are so

important. The world is counting on you and all

your compassion.

Courtney Peppernell

It's the people who have been through so much,

who have lived through moments of trauma and

darkness. They are always the softest, always the

ones that show up for others no matter how they

ache inside. Time and time again they continue

to move through the world, always helping

others. Those are the people I admire most,

those are our real heroes.

Courtney Peppernell

Forge ahead, even when you feel like breaking,

be kind even when your heart is aching.

Courtney Peppernell

I know you have scars, and that others have

opened your heart and caused such chaos inside.

I know how difficult it must be to open your

heart again, to welcome love and all the things

you dread. But I see your worth, and I promise

to be kind instead.

Courtney Peppernell

When I think of her, I think of the wind

softening just to hear her footsteps. I think of

the sky opening and rain falling, just to kiss

her shoulders. I think of the flowers blooming

brighter, just to see her face. Because the earth

always knows kindness and her kindness fills

such a beautiful space.

Courtney Peppernell

I will remember the ones who have asked how

my day was or let me go first in line. I will

remember the ones who have screamed song

lyrics with me, in the front row, even if we had

only just met. I will remember the ones that

have smiled and the one's who have helped me

shine. I will always remember the one's who

have been kind.

Courtney Peppernell

Be someone's lighthouse. Guide their heart with kindness.

Courtney Peppernell

And in those moments where the sun is light

and the sky beautiful, I think about all the

people in the world who need to hear how

beautiful they are.

Because darling; you are, you are, you are.

Courtney Peppernell

You are allowed to walk away from people who

are unkind. You are allowed to seperate yourself

from people who don't have your best interests

at heart. This is your sign, it's your time to start.

Courtney Peppernell

I am choosing to be patient with my choices.

To be kinder to my mistakes. To forgive the

past and let go of old expectations. I am brave

enough to learn, and strong enough to move

forward. And through it all, I will not turn cold

to the world.

Courtney Peppernell

Kindness doesn't always look the same.

Sometimes it is in donations, or scholarships or

running into burning buildings. Other times it is

in quieter moments, like leaving flowers on her

doorstep, reminding someone they have value or

offering up your seat on a busy train. Kindness

is never measured by how big or small the

gesture, it is measured simply by gesturing at all.

Courtney Peppernell

Be someone who treasures every moment, who feels things deeply. Be someone who is considerate and kind and gentle. Someone who tips their waiter a little more, who holds open the door, who gives without expecting anything in return. Be someone who isn't afraid to be sensitive or read poetry or tell a stranger to have a good day. Be someone who loves the people they care about and tells them every other day. Be someone the world needs more of.

Courtney Peppernell

Of all the sunsets you see, and the thunder you

hear, of all the flowers you smell, and the freshly

baked bread you taste, of all the hands you

hold, bodies you entwine with, and stories you

fit into; rememeber the greatest sense you will

ever use, is your sense of kindness.

Courtney Peppernell

It's Only
Forever

I just want to know the pattern of your

breathing and how hard your pulse races when

we kiss. I just want to know the touch of your

skin, instead of losing all this sleep.

Courtney Peppernell

She's someone who deserves honesty and

laughter and warm sweaters around her

shoulders, when it's cold. She's someone who

deserves to feel as though she is loved fiercely

and gently at the same time. She is someone

who deserves to go on dates she will remember,

and have her hand held like I will never ever let

go.

Courtney Peppernell

Love speaks so highly of you in my dreams; I am waiting to find you in reality.

She's the smell after rain. She's the burning fire

in my heart. She's the one with golden hair and

glassy eyes like a mid winter sky. She's the old

soul you rarely find. She's the corner of the

library, safe and warm. She's the novel you've

always wanted to read. She's the good morning

you wake up for. She's the breath of fresh air

you've always needed. She's the movie you never

want to end. She's the adventure you dream

about.

Courtney Peppernell

there will be dozens
of people
who will take your
breath away
but the one
who reminds you
to breathe
is the one you
should keep

Courtney Peppernell

No one said love would be easy. But through all

the difficult moments, you have your best friend.

The person who will show up for you time and

time again.

Courtney Peppernell

You are more than the love you have lost.

Courtney Peppernell

I think you are beautiful for wanting to always

help others. For dreaming of how to make the

world better. I think the way you smile and the

way you speak and hold yourself is enough to

make me weak.

There will come a day, where someone comes

along and while you only ask for a star, they

bring you the whole universe.

Courtney Peppernell

I hope with all my heart, for all my life that you

find your worth. That you learn to love

yourself. That you find your forever home, that

you achieve your dreams, and that happiness

settles deep into your veins. I hope you find the

love of your life and get to see the places you

have always wanted to see. I hope you recover,

embrace your flaws and stay strong. I hope

with everything that I have, you find where you

belong.

Courtney Peppernell

Despite the heartache, the pain, the trauma and the sacrifice, you have to believe you will come out the other side. You have to focus on overcoming the mountain, of rising to start a new day, of taking back your place and throne in life. You have to picture all the good things that will come your way; the picnic by the ocean, a place to call home, a friend or love that makes you feel less alone. You have to hold on and look towards the hope.

Courtney Peppernell

This poetry book was created with the intent to raise money for injured wildlife and assist communities affected by the 2019/2020 nation-wide Australian bushfires.
A percentage of all profits will be donated to WIRES AUSTRALIA to assist in the ongoing relief efforts. Thank you for your contribution and please keep Australian rural communities, firefighters, volunteers, families and wildlife in your thoughts.

follow along on instagram
@courtneypeppernell

FOR MORE WAYS TO HELP VISIT:
www.wires.org.au

ISBN: 9781656327796

Printed by Amazon Italia Logistica S.r.l.
Torrazza Piemonte (TO), Italy